P9-CBC-857

HANA SHAULOV
JEWISH HOLIDAY CAKES

KOSHER

ADAMA BOOKS, NEW YORK

TABLE OF CONTENTS

INTRODUCTION

Jewish holidays are family occasions, and a homemade cake is the ideal way to end a festive dinner or an afternoon get-together. As each holiday approaches, the hostess tries to find new recipes, and new cakes typical of the particular holiday.

This book contains over seventy Holiday cake recipes. The cakes are all traditional and do not use any substitutes or mixes. Some Jewish holidays are associated with various tastes and ingredients. Rosh Hashanah is characterized by honey. Ground poppy seeds are used on Purim, cheese is typical of Shavuot and cakes baked without flour are served during Passover.

However, some festive occasions are celebrated outside, where family and friends gather. In the chapter dealing with Sukkot I have included cakes that are easy to cut and serve in the Sukkah, or "hut" in which the holiday is traditionally celebrated. The cakes in the chapter dealing with Independence Day are suitable for picnics as well as parties.

And, of course, there are the holidays which are not traditionally Jewish. Many children wonder what to prepare for Mother's Day, and everyone is always on the look-out for new ideas for birthday cakes. The chapter titled "Special Occasions" was added for this purpose, and includes various ideas for festive, easy-to-make cakes. Remember, you can bake every cake in this book for all occasions. The chocolate cake in the last chapter, for instance, is suitable for Passover since it does not contain flour. All the cakes in the book are ideal for afternoon coffee or a lazy Sunday afternoon, so leaf through the book before you decide on which cake to prepare.

The color photographs demonstrate how the finished cake should look, but they should be used as general guidelines. Let your imagination run free, and practice the variations included in the recipes.

Bon Appetit!

Hana Shaulov

TIPS AND BASIC RULES

■ *For glazing a cake with jam, always use a slightly sour jam, such as apricot. For easier spreading, slightly heat it in a small saucepan before using.*

■ *Always use the kind of nuts specified in the recipe – walnuts, pecans or hazelnuts – unless the recipe expressly states that they can be substituted for each other. When recipe calls for "plain chocolate" use either milk chocolate or special dark chocolate candy bars.*

■ *Individual oven temperatures vary slightly from one oven to another. Therefore the temperatures in this book are approximate and the terms refer to the following temperatures*

Low – 200–250° F
Medium – 300–350° F
High – 400–450° F

■ *When baking a yeast cake, allow time for rising. In several recipes the dough includes yeast but is not allowed to rise. The resulting pastry resembles sweet shortcrust pastry. To enable yeast dough to rise (unless otherwise specified in the recipe), prepare as follows:*

Dissolve the yeast in a little lukewarm water and immediately add the sugar. Stir well and set aside for about 10 minutes, or until mixture bubbles and rises.

Blend the yeast mixture with the rest of the ingredients and knead well until dough is smooth, firm and does not stick. Cover with a clean dish towel and leave to rise in a warm spot for about 1½ hours, or until dough doubles its volume.

Shape the cake or doughnuts as specified and continue according to recipe.

Yeast in granular form comes in envelopes and need not be set aside to prove before using, and thus the first stage may be omitted. Cake yeast, which must be refrigerated, must be allowed to prove as described above.

ROSH HASHANAH

LIGHT HONEY CAKE

INGREDIENTS:

4 eggs, separated
½ cup sugar
1 tablespoon oil
1 tablespoon brandy
1 cup honey
1 teaspoon ground cinnamon
½ teaspoon ground cloves
1½ cups self-rising flour
1 teaspoon baking soda
Juice of 1 small lemon

Powdered sugar to decorate

A round 10 inch cake tin

Preheat oven to a medium temperature (350°).
Beat the egg whites, gradually adding the sugar, until stiff.
In a mixing bowl, put the egg yolks with the oil, brandy, honey and spices and stir gently, using a wooden spoon.
Fold the yolk mixture gently into the beaten egg whites. Mix the flour with the baking soda and sprinkle on the mixture together with the lemon juice and fold till no traces of flour remain and the batter is uniform. Pour the batter into the greased tin and bake in preheated oven for 40–50 minutes.
When cake is baked, sprinkle with powdered sugar.

CRUMBLY HONEY CAKE

INGREDIENTS:

5 eggs, separated
¾ cup sugar
¼ cup oil
¾ cup honey
1¾ cups self-rising flour
1 teaspoon cinnamon
½ teaspoon ground cloves
vanilla to taste

A round 10 inch cake tin or a loaf
  tin

Preheat oven to a medium temperature (350°).
Beat the egg whites, gradually adding the sugar,
until stiff.
Add the egg yolks and the oil to the beaten egg
whites and stir gently with a wooden spoon.
Slowly add the honey to the mixture, stirring all
the time, then fold in the spices, vanilla and
flour.
Pour into the greased tin and bake in preheated
oven for 45–55 minutes.

HONEY BUNS

INGREDIENTS:

*These are round muffins which
do not contain eggs and are best
eaten on the day they are made.
If you do not own a muffin tin
bake them in paper cases.*

*4 tablespoons oil
2 cups honey
1 cup sugar
Pinch of ground cinnamon
Pinch of ground cloves
Pinch of ground nutmeg
1 cup hot chocolate (made of 1
   teaspoon unsweetened cocoa
   powder, 1 cup hot water and 2
   teaspoons sugar)
2 oz. seedless raisins
6 oz. almonds, finely chopped
4 cups self-rising flour*

*2 large muffin tins
Makes about 24 muffins*

*Preheat oven to a medium temperature (325°).
Put the oil, honey and sugar in a medium
saucepan and heat, over a low flame, until
sugar is dissolved. Leave to cool a little.
Add the cinnamon, ground cloves, nutmeg, the
cup of hot chocolate, raisins and almonds and
mix well. Finally, stir in the flour.
Grease and flour the muffin tin, pour the batter
into the tin and bake in preheated oven for 20
minutes, or until cakes are golden and springy
to the touch.*

BRANDY AND ALMOND HONEY CAKE

INGREDIENTS:

6½ oz. butter or margarine
¾ cup sugar
3 eggs
⅓ cup honey
⅔ cup strawberry jam
½ teaspoon ground cloves
½ teaspoon ground cinnamon
¼ cup brandy
1 cup hot chocolate (made of 1
    teaspoon unsweetened cocoa
    powder, 1 cup boiling water
    and 2 teaspoons sugar)
3⅓ cups self-rising flour

To garnish:
½ cup almonds, shelled, roasted
    and halved

1 large loaf tin or 2 small ones

Preheat oven to a medium temperature (325°).
In the mixer bowl, beat the butter or margarine with the sugar until light and fluffy.
Beat in the eggs, one after the other. Add the honey, jam, cloves, cinnamon and brandy and mix well. Alternately add the flour and the hot chocolate, beating well after each addition.
Line the tin with wax paper and pour in the batter. Bake in preheated oven for 1–1¼ hours (1¼ hours if using a large tin; 1 hour if using 2 small ones.)
About 10 minutes before the cake is done sprinkle the halved almonds on top.

APPLE PIE WITH WHIPPED CREAM

INGREDIENTS:

Pastry:
1½ cups self-rising flour
¼ cup sugar
3½ oz. butter or margarine
1 tablespoon brandy
1 egg yolk

Filling:
3 lbs. cooking apples, peeled and
  cored
½ cup sugar (to cook apples)
cinnamon to taste
2 oz. chopped walnuts
3½ oz. seedless raisins
juice of 1 small lemon
⅛ cup sweet red wine
1 cup whipping cream
1–2 tablespoons sugar (to
  sweeten cream)

A rectangular 9x13 inch cake tin

Preheat the oven to a medium temperature 350°).
Put flour and sugar in a mixing bowl. Add the butter or margarine, brandy and the egg yolk and knead to a smooth dough.
Grease the cake tin. Roll out the dough and line the base and sides of the tin. Bake for about 15 minutes, or until the pastry shell is well cooked and golden. Remove from oven.
Slice apples thinly, put in a saucepan and add the ½ cup sugar. Cook over a low flame, stirring all the time.
Add the cinnamon, walnuts and raisins and cook uncovered, until the apples are softened. You may add a little water only if the apples are not juicy enough.
Mix the lemon juice and the wine and sprinkle the mixture on the baked shell.
Arrange the cooked apples thickly on the pastry shell.
Beat the cream, gradually adding the sugar, until it holds in soft peaks. Spread the cream on the apple filling and refrigerate.

NO-HONEY HONEY CAKE

INGREDIENTS:

Not everyone likes the taste of honey, but a dark, spicey cake is a must for the New Year. This is just such a cake, and it substitutes apricot jam for the honey.

1½ cups sugar
2 cups cold milk
2 eggs
3½ cups self-rising flour
1 teaspoon ground cloves
1 tablespoon ground cinnamon
2 tablespoons cocoa powder,
   unsweetened
½ cup apricot jam
3½ oz. nuts, chopped
3½ oz. seedless raisins
6 dried apricots, chopped
   (optional)

A round 10 inch cake tin

Preheat the oven to a medium temperature (350°).
Put 1 cup of sugar in a large saucepan and heat over a low flame until it caramelizes. Add the milk and stir. When the caramel is melted add the rest of the sugar and leave to cool.
Add the eggs, flour, ground cloves, cinnamon, cocoa powder and the jam and mix well. Finally, add the nuts, raisins and apricots (if using).
Pour batter into a slightly greased baking tin and bake in preheated oven for about 40–50 minutes.

SUKKOT

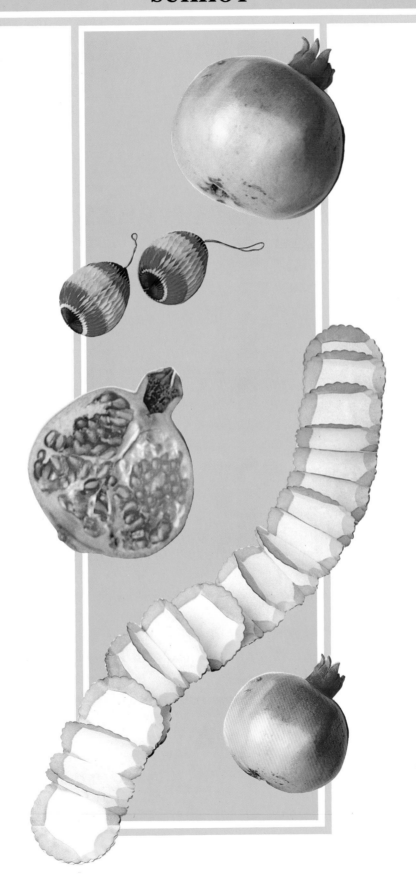

DATE STRUDEL

Pastry:
2½ cups self-rising flour
⅔ cup sour cream
6½ oz. butter or margarine

Filling:
12 oz. date spread or lekvar
1 lb. dates, chopped
½ teaspoon cinnamon or to taste
½ cup sugar or to taste
3½ oz. nuts, chopped (walnuts,
    pecans or hazelnuts)
powdered sugar

A shallow, rectangular baking tin
    or large cookie sheet

Preheat the oven to a medium temperature (350°).

In a mixing bowl, knead together flour, cream and butter or margarine to a soft, smooth dough.

Divide the dough into three parts and roll each out thinly. Spread each part of the dough with a third of the date spread, cover with a third of the chopped dates and sprinkle cinnamon, sugar and a third of the nuts on top.

Grease the baking tin. Roll up each dough sheet lengthwise to form the strudel. Pinch edges tightly to seal and place in the tin.

Bake in preheated oven for about 25 minutes, or until cakes are golden. Remove from oven, let cool and sprinkle with powdered sugar.

CHOCOLATE PIE

INGREDIENTS:

Pastry:
3½ oz. butter or margarine
¼ cup sugar
1 tablespoon brandy
1 egg yolk
1½ cups self-rising flour

Filling:
1 12 oz. package chocolate chips
½ cup sugar
6 tablespoons water
1 teaspoon vanilla
5 eggs, separated
3½ oz. nuts, chopped
1½ tablespoons brandy
1 tablespoon sugar
Juice of 1 small lemon

A rectangular 10x13 inch baking
   tin

Preheat oven to a medium temperature (350°).

In a mixing bowl, combine the pastry ingredients and knead to a smooth dough (the dough can also be kneaded in a mixer).

Line the bottom of a baking tin or cookie sheet with the dough and bake in preheated oven for about 15 minutes.

While shell is baking, prepare the filling: put the chocolate chips, ¼ cup of sugar and 6 tablespoons water in a saucepan placed over a pot of boiling water and heat until melted. Leave to cool.

Add the vanilla. Beat the egg yolks and add to the chocolate. Stir until mixture thickens.

Beat the egg whites to a froth, then gradually add a ¼ cup of sugar, beating all the time, until the foam holds stiff peaks.

Gently fold the chocolate mixture into the beaten egg whites, using a wooden spoon, until no trace of the whites remains. Fold in the nuts.

In a cup, blend the brandy, remaining tablespoon of sugar and a little lemon juice. Stir and sprinkle on the baked pastry shell.

Pour the chocolate filling in the pastry shell and refrigerate.

LEMON MERINGUE PIE

INGREDIENTS:

Pastry:
3½ oz. butter
½ cup water
2 cups plain flour (more may be
  added, if needed)

Filling:
1½ cups water
1 oz. margarine
4 tablespoons cornstarch or
  lemon flavored custard powder
1½ cups sugar
3 eggs, separated
½ cup lemon juice

A deep round 10 inch cake tin or
  a small, square 10x10 inch tin

Preheat oven to a medium temperature (350°).
Knead all pastry ingredients to a smooth dough.
Grease the tin and line bottom and sides with an even layer of dough.

Prick bottom of pastry shell with a fork and bake in preheated oven for 15–20 minutes, or until the pastry is golden-brown. Remove from the oven and leave to cool.

While pastry is baking, prepare the lemon filling: in a saucepan, put 1 cup of water and the margarine. Bring to a boil.

In a cup, combine the cornstarch or the custard powder with remaining ½ cup of water and stir well. Add to boiling mixture in saucepan, stir well and bring again to a boil. Remove from flame and cook till it thickens.

Gradually add 1¼ cups of the sugar, the egg yolks and the lemon juice and stir to a smooth mixture. Pour into cooled shell.

Beat the egg whites with remaining ¼ cup of sugar until stiff. Pour the beaten egg whites on top of the filling and bake in low heat for 10 minutes, or until meringue is golden.

VANILLA AND RASPBERRY PRESERVE PIE

INGREDIENTS:

Pastry:
1½ cups plain flour
3½ oz. margarine
1 egg
2 tablespoons sugar

Filling:
4 cups milk
½ cup sugar
½ cup plain flour
1 tablespoon vanilla
3 egg yolks

Topping:
1 cup raspberry preserve

A 10 inch pie dish

Preheat oven to a medium temperature (350°).
In a bowl, combine all pastry ingredients and knead to a smooth dough. Roll dough out, on a floured board, to a circle to fit a 10 inch pie dish. Grease the bottom and sides of dish.
Wrap dough loosely around the rolling pin and transfer to the dish. Prick the bottom of the dough with a fork, to prevent it from rising.
Bake in preheated oven for 25 minutes, until pale golden. Remove from oven and cool.
While pastry is baking, prepare the filling: in a saucepan, combine the milk, sugar, flour and vanilla. Bring to a boil, stirring constantly.
After mixture has reached boiling point, stir for 5 more minutes and remove from flame. Stir in the egg yolks and pour into cooled shell.
Allow the filling time to set. When set, spread on the raspberry preserve. If preserve is too thick for easy spreading, heat it a little in a small saucepan. Store in refrigerator.

NAPOLEON WITH CREAM FILLING

INGREDIENTS:

This cake has to be prepared a day in advance.

Pastry:
1 egg
1/2 cup sugar
3 1/2 oz. butter, softened
1 1/2 cups self-rising flour
5 oz. hazelnuts, roasted and ground
1 teaspoon vanilla

Cream Filling:
7 egg yolks
3/4 cup sugar
1/3 cup milk
1/8 cup hot milk (to dissolve gelatine)
1/2 oz. unflavored gelatine
2 cups whipping cream

Topping:
1 cup whipping cream

A square 18x18 inch baking tin or 2 7x11 inch baking tins

Preheat oven to a high temperature (375°).
Combine pastry ingredients in a mixing bowl and knead to a smooth dough. Line a large, square baking tin with greased wax paper. Roll out the pastry thinly and line bottom of prepared tin. With the tip of a knife, score a deep line dividing the pastry in two. Bake for several minutes, or until pastry is pale golden. Remove from oven, divide into two leaves along scored line and leave to cool.

Prepare the cream: *in a small saucepan, place the yolks, sugar and 1/3 cup milk. Place saucepan on top of a pan of boiling water and cook over a low flame. Beat with an electric hand mixer while mixture cooks, until it coats the back of a wooden spoon.*
Meanwhile, sprinkle the gelatine on the hot milk and stir until completely dissolved. Gradually pour into the yolk mixture, stirring all the time, until mixture is smooth. Beat the whipping cream till it holds its shape. Gently fold the cooked yolk mixture into the whipped cream. Spread the cream filling on one pastry layer and cover with the second.
Beat the remaining cup of whipping cream till it holds its shape and spread on top. Chill for 24 hours, then serve.

32

CHOCOLATE CREAM FILLED SANDWICHES

INGREDIENTS:

Pastry:
1 egg
½ cup sugar
3½ oz. margarine
1¾ cups self-rising flour
Wax paper

Filling:
5 oz. butter, softened
6½ oz. powdered sugar
1 teaspoon cocoa powder,
*   unsweetened*

Chcolate Glaze:
6 oz. chocolate chips
2 oz. butter

A rectangular 9½x13½ cookie
*   sheet*

Preheat oven to a medium temperature (350°).
Knead all pastry ingredients together to a soft dough.
Line tin with wax paper and spread the dough on it evenly and thinly. Using a 3 inch pastry cutter, mark circles in dough.
Bake in preheated oven for 15–20 minutes, or until the pastry is pale golden. Remove from oven and leave to cool. When pastry has cooled, remove the circles carefully from tin (the leftovers can be used to make chocolate truffles).
To make the filling: *Beat the butter and powdered sugar together with a wooden spoon. Sift the cocoa powder to remove any lumps and beat into the butter cream. Spread some of the cream on one of the baked circles and cover with another circle. Sandwich together the rest of the circles.*
To make chocolate glaze: *in a saucepan, put the chocolate and margarine. Stir over a low flame until melted, and spread on top of the cakes. Store in refrigerator.*

HANUKAH

EASY-TO-MAKE DOUGHNUTS

INGREDIENTS:

2½ cups plain flour
2 egg yolks
1½ tablespoons sugar
1 oz. margarine
1 tablespoon vanilla
¾ cup lukewarm milk
½ oz. yeast, dissolved in a little
   warm milk
Jam for filling
Oil for deep frying

Makes about 15 doughnuts

In a mixing bowl place the flour, egg yolks, sugar, margarine, vanilla, milk and dissolved yeast. Knead to a smooth and elastic dough. Cover and let rise in a warm place for about 1½ hours, or until dough doubles its volume.
Roll out to a circle about ½ an inch thick. With a 2 inch pastry cutter cut out circles, cover and let rise again.
Heat oil to medium hot. Drop risen doughnuts into oil, cover and cook for 1 minute. When doughnuts are golden on one side, uncover pan and turn over. When both sides are done, remove with a slotted spoon and drain on kitchen paper. Inject warmed jam into doughnuts and sprinkle with powdered sugar.

DULCE DE LECHE CHOCOLATE DOUGHNUTS

INGREDIENTS:

Dulce de Leche is an Argentinian jam, made of caramelized sugar and milk. It can be obtained in Cuban specialty stores.

For Doughnuts:
2 oz. yeast
A little lukewarm milk
A pinch of sugar
6½ cups plain flour
6 tablespoons sugar
2 scant teaspoons salt
3 whole eggs
2 egg yolks
2 tablespoons brandy
1 teaspoon vanilla
5 oz. margarine, cubed
1½ cups lukewarm milk
Oil for deep frying

Filling:
1 cup Dulce de Leche

Chocolate Glaze:
½ cup water
½ cup sugar
6½ oz. plain chocolate
1½ tablespoons cocoa powder, unsweetened

Makes about 20 doughnuts

Dissolve the yeast in a little milk, add a pinch of sugar and leave in a draft-free place until mixture froths.

Place the flour in a bowl, make a well in the center and put in the sugar and salt. Pour into the well the dissolved yeast, eggs, egg yolks, brandy, vanilla and margarine. Beat, gradually adding the milk, until mixture forms a soft dough. Knead lightly by hand, cover the bowl with a clean dish-towel and leave in a warm spot until dough doubles its volume.

Roll out dough on a floured board to a circle about 1 inch thick and cut out circles with a 2 inch pastry cutter. Let rise for about 15 minutes. Heat the oil to medium (not smoking) hot. Drop doughnuts into the oil, cover pan and fry for 1 minute. Remove lid, turn doughnuts over and fry a further minute. Remove from oil and drain on kitchen paper. Inject with warmed Dulce de Leche.

To make chocolate glaze: *place the water and sugar in a saucepan. Stir over a low flame until sugar is dissolved. Stir in the chocolate. Add the cocoa powder and stir until glaze is slightly thickened. Pour the glaze on the doughnuts.*

BULGARIAN BEIGNETS

INGREDIENTS:

4 cups plain flour
1 oz. yeast
3 cups lukewarm water
Pinch of salt
Oil for deep frying

Syrup:
3 cups sugar
1½ cups water
juice of half a lemon
1 scant teaspoon ground
  cinnamon

Makes about 15 beignets

Place the flour in a mixing bowl. Dissolve the yeast in a cup of lukewarm water and add to the flour. Beat well, by hand or using a hand mixer, gradually adding the remaining 2 cups of water. Add the salt and keep beating to a smooth, soft dough.

Cover with a clean dish towel and let rise in a warm place for about an hour.

When dough is well risen, heat the oil in a deep-fryer. Tear out pieces of the dough and drop into hot oil. Turn beignets over and fry until golden on both sides. Remove with a slotted spoon and drain on kitchen paper.

To make Syrup: Put sugar, water and lemon juice in a saucepan. Cook over a low flame for about 20 minutes, add cinnamon and stir well.

Dip beignets in prepared syrup and serve immediately.

JELLY DOUGHNUTS

INGREDIENTS:

Remember, the oil for frying can be strained and used again – a handy tip, since Hanukah is eight days long.
If using granular yeast, it need not be set aside to prove before using.

6½ cups plain flour (about 1⅔ lbs.)
7 tablespoons sugar
1½ cups lukewarm milk
2 oz. yeast
2 whole eggs
2 egg yolks
2 tablespoons brandy
1 teaspoon vanilla
5 oz. margarine, cubed
2 scant teaspoons salt
Oil for deep frying
Jam for filling

Makes about 20 doughnuts

Place flour in mixing bowl, make a well in the center and add the sugar and salt.

In a separate bowl dissolve yeast in a little lukewarm milk (about ¼ cup), add a pinch of sugar and set aside until mixture bubbles and rises. Add the yeast mixture to the flour, then add the eggs, yolks, brandy, vanilla, margarine and salt.

Beat for 5–7 minutes, gradually adding the milk. Cover and let rise for 1–1½ hours. Flour a board and divide the risen dough into two parts. Roll out each part to a ½ inch thick circle. Cut out circles, using a 2 inch pastry cutter. Let rise, covered, on a floured tray for about 20 minutes.

Pour about 12 cups of oil into a large pot. Heat, but make sure the oil is not boiling hot. Drop risen doughnuts into hot oil, cover and fry for 1 minute. Remove lid, turn doughnuts over and fry, uncovered, for a further minute until the doughnuts are golden-brown. Remove with a slotted spoon and drain on kitchen paper.

Before serving, inject warmed jam into every doughnut and sprinkle with sugar.

WALNUT AND CREAM CAKE

INGREDIENTS:

The cake is prepared in two stages: The whipped cream and chocolate are cooked and chilled for 24 hours. The next day the cake is baked and covered with the whipped chocolate cream.

Chocolate Cream:
6 oz. chocolate chips
2 cups whipping cream

Cake:
6 tablespoons brandy
½ cup milk
1 tablespoon instant coffee powder
3 tablespoons cocoa powder
1 cup sugar
¾ cups self-rising flour
5 eggs
2 0z. Walnuts, finely chopped
2 tablespoons oil

Glaze:
½ cup apricot jam

A round 10 inch cake tin

To make chocolate cream, place the cream and chocolate chips in a small saucepan and stir over a low flame, until mixture is smooth and uniform. Heat till just below boiling point, remove from flame and stir to dissolve all chocolate. Store overnight in refrigerator.

The next day, preheat oven to a medium temperature (350°).

In a saucepan, cook the brandy, milk, instant coffee powder and cocoa powder, stirring all the time. Gradually add 3 tablespoons of the sugar and 1 tablespoon of the flour and continue cooking until mixture thickens. Remove from flame and let cool.

Meanwhile, beat the eggs and the rest of the sugar at a high speed for about 7 minutes, until pale and thick. Fold in the hazelnuts, oil, remaining flour and the cocoa mixture. Pour into a greased tin and bake for about 40 minutes. Let cool and chill for several hours.

Beat the chilled chocolate cream until it holds in soft peaks. Halve the cake and spread half of the apricot jam on the bottom half. On the jam half spread half of the chocolate cream and cover with the top half of the cake. Cover the sides and top of the cake with remaining jam and chocolate cream.

MOROCCAN BEIGNETS

INGREDIENTS:

4½ cups plain flour
Lukewarm water (as much as
    needed)
2 tablespoons sugar
½ oz. yeast, dissolved in a little
    lukewarm milk
Pinch of salt
Oil for deep frying

Makes about 20 beignets

In a mixing bowl, blend flour and water to a
pouring cream consistency. Add the sugar,
yeast and salt.
Cover with a clean dish-towel and let rise in a
warm place for 1–1½ hours.
Heat oil in a deep-fryer. Wet hands, tear out a
golf-ball sized piece of the dough and, using the
other hand, punch a hole in the center of the
chunk of dough. This must be done quickly.
Drop the beignets into the hot oil and fry until
golden brown. Remove with a slotted spoon,
drain on kitchen paper, sprinkle with powdered
sugar and serve warm.

QUICK AND EASY CREAM DOUGHNUTS

INGREDIENTS:

These doughnuts must be fried until well browned in hot, but not smoking, oil. If the oil is too hot they will brown too quickly on the outside, leaving the inside uncooked.

1 cup whipping cream
2 eggs
Pinch of salt
3 teaspoons powdered sugar
2½ cups plain flour
2 teaspoons baking powder
1 tablespoon brandy
Oil for frying

To Decorate:
Powdered sugar

Makes about 20 doughnuts

Mix all ingredients together.
Heat oil in a deep fryer. Pour batter into hot oil, using a spoon, and fry on both sides to a golden brown.
Remove with a slotted spoon, drain on kitchen paper and leave to cool. Sprinkle with powdered sugar before serving.

TU B'SHVAT

APPLE AND RAISIN CAKE

INGREDIENTS:

6 cooking apples, peeled and
   cored
1¼ cups sugar
1–2 teaspoons ground cinnamon
4 eggs
¾ cup oil
3 cups self-rising flour
Juice of 1 large lemon
3½ oz. seedless raisins
2 oz. chocolate chips
10 candied cherries (optional)

Powdered sugar for sprinkling

A round 10 inch cake tin or a
   large loaf tin

Preheat oven to a medium temperature (350°).
Slice the apples thinly, sprinkle on the slices ¼ cup of the sugar and cinnamon to taste and set aside for 15 minutes.
Beat the eggs with the rest of the sugar until pale and thick. Gradually beat in the oil, flour and lemon juice.
Transfer ¾ of the batter to a greased tin. Arrange the apple slices, raisins, chocolate chips and cherries (if using) on the batter in the tin and pour remaining batter on top.
Bake in preheated oven for 40–60 minutes, or until done.
Remove from oven, leave to cool, turn out and sprinkle with powdered sugar.

DRIED FRUIT CAKE

INGREDIENTS:

6½ oz. margarine, softened
1¼ cups sugar
4 eggs
3 cups self-rising flour
5 oz. seedless raisins
3½ oz. dried apricots, chopped
2 tablespoons lemon juice

A round 10 inch cake tin or a
*   large loaf tin*

Preheat oven to a medium temperature (350°).
In the mixer bowl, beat the margarine and sugar at minimum speed, until light and fluffy.
Gradually add the eggs, one at a time, beating after each addition.
Place the flour, raisins and apricots in a mixing bowl and mix well. Fold into the batter.
Sprinkle the lemon juice on the batter and beat well. Gently pour into greased tin and bake in preheated oven for about 40 minutes.

RICH DATE CAKE

INGREDIENTS:

Line the tin with wax paper, to prevent sticking. The cake does not rise very high, so for best results bake a large, flat cake, cut in half and sandwich together with cream. The batter can also be baked in two separate tins. If baked in two tins, grease and flour one tin, and line the second with wax paper. When the second cake is baked it can be placed on top of the first cake. If using a single tin, it should only be greased and floured.

Cake Batter:
5–6 egg whites
1¼ cups sugar
6½ oz. hazelnuts, ground
8 oz. dates, cut lengthwise into
  strips
2 tablespoons breadcrumbs
1 tablespoon vanilla

Filling:
2 cups whipping cream
2 tablespoons sugar

A 9½x13½ inch cookie sheet or
  two loaf tins

Preheat oven to a low temperature (275°).
Beat the egg whites to a foam, gradually add the sugar and continue beating until stiff.
In a separate bowl mix hazelnuts, dates and breadcrumbs. Fold carefully into beaten egg whites, using a wooden spoon.
Add vanilla and stir gently. Pour the batter into prepared tins and bake in preheated oven for 1 hour until set. If using a single square tin, cut baked cake lengthwise . Let cool.
Beat the whipping cream till it holds its shape, gradually adding the sugar. Sandwich cakes together using half of the cream, then cover with remaining cream.

RAISIN AND NUT CAKE

INGREDIENTS:

4 eggs, separated
1 cup sugar
6½ oz. margarine, softened
8 oz. cream cheese
1 tablespoon lemon juice
2 oz. nuts, chopped
5 dried dates, finely chopped
3½ oz. raisins
3 cups self-rising flour

2 loaf tins or a 10 inch round
    cake tin

Preheat oven to a medium temperature (350°).
Beat the egg whites, gradually adding the sugar, until stiff.
In a separate bowl, beat the margarine, cheese and the egg yolks until smooth. Beat in the lemon juice, nuts, dates and raisins.
Gently fold the cheese mixture into the beaten egg whites, using a wooden spoon, until no trace of the whites remains. Finally, fold in the flour.
Pour batter into 2 greased loaf tins, or 1 round 10 inch tin and bake for about 40 minutes.

DRIED FRUIT STRUDEL

INGREDIENTS:

Pastry:
3 cups self-rising flour
2/3 cup sour cream
6 1/2 oz. margarine

Filling:
6 oz. seedless raisins
6 oz. nuts, chopped
6 oz. dried figs, chopped
5 oz. dried apricots, chopped
6 dried dates, chopped
3 1/2 oz. candied cherries,
*   chopped*
4 cups desiccated coconut
1 cup sugar
Cinnamon to taste
1 small jar apricot jam

A large, shallow baking sheet

Preheat oven to a medium temperature (350°).
Combine all pastry ingredients in a mixing bowl and knead to a smooth dough. Divide dough into four parts.
In a separate bowl, mix all filling ingredients, except the jam, and divide into 4 equal portions.
On a floured board, roll out thinly each portion of the dough. Spread each portion with a quarter of the jam.
Sprinkle each portion of the dough with a portion of the filling mixture, roll up to make the strudel and place all four strudels on one large, greased baking sheet.
Bake in preheated oven for about 30 minutes. When baked cut into slices, leave to cool and sprinkle with powdered sugar.

DATE AND APRICOT CAKE

INGREDIENTS:

5 medium eggs, separated
½ cup oil
3 cups self-rising flour
6 oz. pecan nuts, chopped
3½ oz. dried apricots, chopped
1 lb. dried dates, pitted and
   chopped
1 cup sugar

A large loaf tin or 2 small loaf
   pans

Preheat oven to a medium temperature (350°).
In a mixing bowl, beat together egg yolks and oil to a smooth mixture.
In a separate bowl, blend the flour and nuts, then add the apricots and dates.
Fold the flour mixture into the yolks.
Beat the egg whites, gradually adding the sugar, until stiff.
Gently fold the beaten egg whites into the flour and yolk mixture, and continue folding to a light, uniform batter.
Grease a loaf tin, or line with wax paper. Pour batter into prepared tin and bake in heated oven for about 40 minutes.

ORANGE AND RAISIN CAKE

INGREDIENTS:

Cake:
2 cups self-rising flour
2 oz. nuts, chopped
2 oz. seedless raisins
5 eggs
1½ cups sugar
½ cup oil
1 cup orange juice
1 tablespoon vanilla
1 tablespoon cornstarch

Butter Cream:
6½ oz. butter or margarine
6½ oz. powdered sugar

To Decorate:
Candied friut

2 loaf tins or a round 10 inch
   cake tin

Preheat oven to a medium temperature (350°).
In a mixing bowl, blend flour with nuts and raisins.
In a mixing bowl, beat the eggs and the sugar at maximum speed for about 10 minutes, until pale and thick.
Reduce mixer speed and add the oil, orange juice, flour mixture and vanilla. Finally, fold in the cornstarch.
Grease the tins and pour the batter into them. Bake in preheated oven for 40–60 minutes. Remove from oven and leave until cooled completely.
When cake is cold, prepare butter cream: beat together the butter and powdered sugar to a smooth cream, spread on top of cake and decorate with candied fruit.

Variation: The batter may be baked in a muffin tin or in paper cases and topped with ready-made chocolate topping and small candies.

PURIM

HAMANTASCHEN

INGREDIENTS:

Poppy seeds are best bought freshly ground.
Prepare the dough a day in advance and chill for 24 hours.

Pastry:
10 oz. margarine, softened
1 whole egg
1 egg yolk
Pinch of salt
1 tablespoon vanilla
1/3 cup sugar
1 oz. yeast
1/4 cup milk
4 cups plain flour
1 teaspoon baking powder

Poppy Seed Filling:
5 oz. poppy seeds, ground
1/2 cup milk
4 tablespoon sugar
2 oz. seedless raisins

For Brushing:
1 egg, beaten

To Decorate:
powdered sugar

In a mixing bowl, beat together the margarine, whole egg, egg yolk, salt, vanilla and sugar until smooth.

Dissolve the yeast in milk and add to the margarine mixture. Stir well. Mix the flour with the baking powder and add to the yeast mixture. Knead to a smooth dough.

Chill dough for 24 hours, then divide into two equal parts.

To make the filling, put all filling ingredients in a small saucepan and cook for several minutes over a low flame, stirring all the time. Set aside to cool.

Preheat oven to a medium temperature (350°).

Roll out each part of the dough and cut out circles, using a 3 inch pastry cutter. Place a heaped teaspoon of the filling in the center of each circle and close up to form a triangle. Pinch edges tightly, to prevent them opening during baking.

Brush with beaten egg and bake in preheated oven for about 20 minutes, or until pale golden. Remove from oven, let cool and sprinkle with powdered sugar.

FESTIVE POPPYSEED CAKE

INGREDIENTS:

6 eggs
1½ cups sugar
2 tablespoons oil
1 tablespoon brandy
2 tablespoons breadcrumbs
3½ oz. nuts, chopped
3½ oz. seedless raisins
3½ oz. poppy seeds, ground

A round 10 inch cake tin

Preheat oven to a medium temperature (350°).
In the mixer bowl, beat the eggs and sugar at maximum speed until pale and thick (about 10 minutes).
Using a wooden spoon, fold in the oil, brandy, breadcrumbs, nuts, raisins and ground poppy seeds.
Pour the batter into a greased tin and bake in preheated oven for about 35 minutes. Remove fron oven and leave to cool.

Variation: Cream topping – beat 1 cup whipping cream and 1 tablespoon sugar until stiff. Spread warmed apricot jam on top of cake and spread the whipped cream on top.

POPPYSEED HAMANTASCHEN

INGREDIENTS:

Filling:*
12 oz. poppy seeds, ground
½ cup sugar (or to taste)
2 tablespoons honey
2 oz. seedless raisins
⅓-½ cup milk
1 tablespoon breadcrumbs
1 tablespoon margarine

*Or fill with Solo Poppy Filling
mixed with raisins and honey to
taste

Pastry:
2 oz. yeast
2 lbs. plain flour
½ cup sugar
Grated rind of 1 lemon
1 lb. margarine
3 eggs
1¾ cups lukewarm water

To make filling, put poppy seeds, sugar, honey, raisins, milk, breadcrumbs and margarine in a small saucepan, bring to a boil and remove from heat. If mixture is too thin cook a minute longer.

To make dough, dissolve the yeast in a little lukewarm water, add 1 teaspoon sugar and set aside until mixture bubbles and rises.

In a bowl, place flour, sugar, lemon rind, margarine, eggs, water and dissolved yeast and knead to a smooth dough.

Cover with a clean dish-towel and let rise in a warm spot until dough doubles its volume.

Preheat oven to a medium temperature (350°).

Roll dough out thickly. Cut out circles, using a 3 inch cookie-cutter. Place a heaped teaspoon of the filling in the center of each circle and fold up to form a triangle. Pinch edges to prevent opening, brush with beaten egg yolk and bake in preheated oven until golden-brown.

CHOCOLATE CREAM PETIT FOURS

INGREDIENTS:

Pastry:
1 egg
½ cup sugar
3½ oz. margarine
2-3 tablespoons cocoa powder,
  unsweetened
1¾ cups plain flour

Cream:
2 cups whipping cream
2 tablespoons sugar
½ teaspoon instant coffee
  powder

A rectangular 12x14 inch baking
  tin or a small cookie sheet

Preheat oven to a medium temperature (350°).
Knead together all pastry ingredients into a smooth dough. Line tin with wax paper and spread dough on the paper lining. With the tip of a knife divide dough into three equal strips, so it can be easily cut after baking.
Bake in preheated oven for about 20 minutes. Remove from oven, leave to cool and carefully turn out of baking tin.
Beat the cream until stiff and add the sugar.
Place one pastry strip on a rectangular cake tray, spread with a third of the whipped cream, cover with a second pastry strip, spread with another third of the cream and finish with the third pastry strip.
Fold the instant coffee powder into the remaining cream, and spread on top of the cake. Chill for 24 hours.
The next day cut into small squares and place in paper cases.
Variation: *The instant coffee powder may be used to flavor all the whipped cream, or omitted.*

CRUMBLY POPPYSEED HAMANTASCHEN

INGREDIENTS:

Filling:
6½ oz. poppy seeds, ground
⅓ cup milk
4 tablespoons sugar
2 oz. seedless raisins
2 tablespoons breadcrumbs

Pastry:
3½ oz. margarine
3½ oz. butter
4 tablespoons oil
¾ cup sugar
2 eggs
1 tablespoon vanilla
4¼ cups plain flour
2½ teaspoons baking powder
½ cup orange juice

A shallow cookie sheet

Place all filling ingredients in a saucepan, stir and cook for 2 minutes, stirring all the time. If too thick, add a little more milk.

In the mixer bowl, beat together at minimum speed the margarine, butter, oil and sugar until smooth.

Gradually add the eggs, one at a time, beating well after each addition, then beat in the vanilla.

Sift together the flour and baking powder. Add, alternately with the orange juice, beating all the time, until a stiff dough is formed. If needed, add a little more flour.

Let dough rest in refrigerator for several hours before using.

Preheat oven to a medium temperature (350°).

Roll dough out on a floured board and cut out circles, using a 3 inch pastry cutter.

Place a teaspoon of the filling in the center of each circle and fold up edges to form triangles. Pinch edges tightly to prevent opening.

Place on a greased cookie sheet and bake in preheated oven for about 25 minutes, or until triangles are lightly browned. Remove from oven and let cool.

To serve, sprinkle with powdered sugar.

POPPYSEED MERINGUE CAKE

INGREDIENTS:

Pastry:
3 cups self-rising flour
3/4 cup sugar
2 eggs
2/3 cup sour cream
3 1/2 oz. margarine

Filling:
1/2 cup milk
5 tablespoons sugar
3 tablespoons margarine
10 oz. poppy seeds, ground
3 1/2 oz. seedless raisins
2 tablespoons brandy
1 egg

Meringue:
3 egg whites
1/2 cup sugar

A round 10-11 inch cake tin

*Preheat oven to a medium temperature (350°).
Knead all pastry ingredients to a smooth dough.
Grease the tin and line bottom and sides with a 1/8 inch layer of dough. (Freeze any leftovers for future use.)
To make filling, place milk, sugar, margarine, poppy seeds, raisins and brandy in a small pan. Cook over a low flame, cool a little, add the egg, stir and leave to cool completely.
Spread the filling on the pastry base and bake in preheated oven for about 25 minutes.
Meanwhile, prepare the meringue – beat the egg whites to a foam, gradually add the sugar and continue beating until stiff.
Remove the cake from oven and reduce oven temperature to low. Spread meringue mixture on filling, return to oven and bake 10-15 minutes more.*

POPPYSEED BUNS

INGREDIENTS:

Dough:
2 oz. yeast
1 cup lukewarm milk
½ cup sugar
½ cup oil
6½ oz. margarine, melted
2 eggs
1 scant teaspoon salt
5 rounded cups plain flour

Filling:*
1 cup poppy seeds, ground
½ cup milk
⅓ cup sugar
1 teaspoon cinnamon
1 tablespoon breadcrumbs

*Or use Solo Poppy Filling

To Decorate:
1 tablespoon cinnamon
½ cup sugar

A large cookie sheet

In a bowl dissolve yeast in milk, add sugar and set aside until mixture bubbles and rises.

Add the oil to the yeast mixture and beat, using a hand mixer at minimum speed.

Gradually add half of the melted margarine, the eggs and salt, beating all the time. Gradually beat in the flour. Continue beating a further 5 minutes, to a smooth, soft dough. Cover and set aside to rise.

Meanwhile, cook the poppy seeds, milk, sugar and cinnamon for about 2 minutes, stirring all the time. Add the breadcrumbs and leave to cool.

In a separate bowl mix sugar and cinnamon.

Preheat oven to a medium temperature (350°).

When dough is well risen, tear out tennis-ball sized chunks and flatten out to a circle. Place a tablespoon of the filling in the center of each circle and pinch edges together to enclose filling.

Dip every cake in remaining melted margarine, then roll in sugar and cinnamon mixture. Arrange the cakes about 3 inches apart on a greased cookie sheet. Bake in preheated oven for about 30 minutes, or until cakes are golden-brown.

PASSOVER

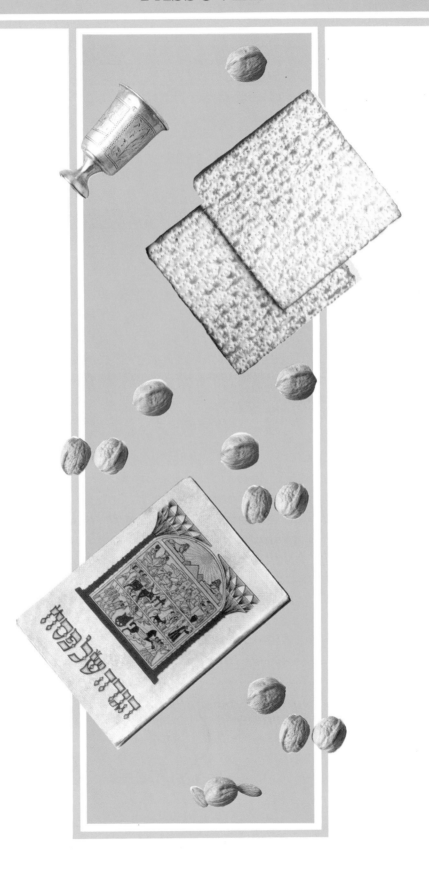

COFFE AND NUT CAKE

INGREDIENTS:

A low, moist cake.

1 large, sweet apple, peeled and cored
6 eggs
1 cup sugar
8 oz. walnuts, finely ground (preferably in a food processor)
2 oz. plain chocolate, grated
1 tablespoon instant coffee powder
2 tablespoons matzoh-meal

To Decorate:
1 cup whipping cream
1 tablespoon sugar, or powdered sugar

A round 10 inch cake tin

Slice the apple thinly, place in a saucepan and cook with a little water for 2–3 minutes, until softened.
Grease tin with a little margarine. Preheat oven to a medium temperature (350°).
In the mixer bowl, place the eggs and the sugar and beat at maximum speed for about 10 minutes, until pale and thick.
Carefully fold in the nuts, grated chocolate, coffee powder and cooked apple, using a wooden spoon. Finally, fold in the matzoh-meal.
Pour batter into a greased tin, bake in preheated oven for about 40 minutes, remove from oven and leave to cool.
To serve, sprinkle with powdered sugar or top with whipped cream:
Beat chilled cream at minimum speed. Gradually add sugar, raise speed of mixer and beat until stiff. Spread on top of cake and store in refrigerator.

PASSOVER CHOCOLATE COOKIES

INGREDIENTS:

4 eggs
2 cups sugar
6½ oz. margarine, melted
1 cup matzoh-meal, finely
  ground
6 tablespoons cocoa powder,
  unsweetened, sifted
5 oz. nuts, chopped
1 tablespoon vanilla

A rectangular 7x11 inch baking
  tin

Preheat oven to a medium temperature (350°).
In a mixing bowl beat together eggs and sugar, using a wooden spoon, until pale and thick.
Beat in melted margarine, matzoh-meal, cocoa powder, nuts and vanilla.
Pour the batter into a greased tin and bake in preheated oven for about 20–30 minutes.
Remove from oven, leave to cool, cut into squares and place in paper cases to serve.

HOLIDAY MERINGUE CAKE

INGREDIENTS:

Meringue:
3 eggs, separated
1 cup sugar

Filling:
6½ oz. butter
6 oz. chocolate chips
2 tablespoons brandy·
2 oz. nuts, chopped
Chocolate syrup to decorate
Wax paper

A square baking tin

Beat the egg whites, gradually adding sugar, until stiff.
Line the tin with wax paper and pour the beaten egg whites into the tin. Bake in an **unpreheated** oven, at a very low heat (200°) for 1½–2 hours.
Remove from oven, let cool a little and turn out. Remove the wax paper and cut the meringue lengthwise. (If meringue breaks the pieces can be rejoined when assembling the cake.)
To make filling, put 2 tablespoons of water, the butter and the chocolate chips in a saucepan. Sti over a low flame until melted.
Add brandy and nuts and stir gently, using a wooden spoon. Let cool, then add the egg yolks one at a time, stirring gently after each addition. Chill mixture, stirring every once in a while, until it thickens.
Place one half of the meringue on a serving dish, spread with the filling then cover with the other half. Decorate with chocolate syrup and chopped nuts, and place in freezer, to set.
The cake·is best prepared several hours ahead and stored in the refrigerator.

NUT AND ALMOND CAKE

INGREDIENTS:

This is a delicious cake, and the cream and jam add to its rich taste.

6 eggs
1¼ cups sugar
5½ oz. almonds, finely ground
3½ oz. walnuts, finely ground
1 tablespoon vanilla
1 tablespoon brandy
1 tablespoon lemon juice
1 tablespoon matzoh-meal
2–3 tablespoons jam
1 cup whipping cream
2 tablespoons sugar

a round 10–11 inch cake tin

Preheat oven to a medium temperature (350°).
Beat the eggs and the sugar, using an electric mixer at maximum speed, until pale and thick (about 10 minutes).
Using a wooden spoon, gently fold in the almonds, walnuts, vanilla, brandy and lemon juice. Finally, fold in the matzoh-meal.
Grease and flour the tin and bake in preheated oven for about 35 minutes. Remove from oven and leave to cool.
Heat the jam and spread it on top of the cake.
Beat the cream, gradually adding the sugar, until stiff and spread on the cake.

MOCHA CREAM CAKE

INGREDIENTS:

¹/₂ cup matzoh-meal
¹/₄ cup potato-flour
3¹/₂ oz. nuts, finely ground
5 eggs
1 cup sugar
2 tablespoons cocoa powder,
  unsweetened, sifted
1 tablespoon instant coffee
  powder
2 oz. plain chocolate, grated
1 tablespoon brandy

Mocha Cream:
5 oz. powdered sugar
3 tablespoons butter, softened
1 teaspoon instant coffee powder
3 tablespoons milk
  (approximately)
1 teaspoon vanilla

A rectangular 11x13 inch baking
  tin or a round 10 inch cake tin

Preheat oven to a medium temperature (350°).
Blend the matzoh-meal and potato flour, then add the ground nuts.
Beat the eggs and sugar, using an electric mixer at maximum speed, until thick and pale (about 7 minutes).
Using a wooden spoon, fold in the matzoh-meal and nut mixture, cocoa powder, instant coffee powder, grated chocolate and brandy.
Pour batter into greased tin and bake in preheated oven for about 40 minutes. Remove cake from oven and leave to cool.
To make mocha cream, beat together all ingredients to a smooth cream. Put cream in a piping bag fitted with a star nozzle and pipe rosettes on top of the cake.

NUT CAKE

INGREDIENTS:

5 eggs
¾ cup sugar
5 oz. hazelnuts, ground
5 oz. plain chocolate, grated
¾ cup matzoh-meal*
1 teaspoon baking powder
1 tablespoon brandy
¼ cup orange juice, freshly
 squeezed or canned

*Available before Passover in
Jewish specialty stores

Powdered sugar

A round 10 inch cake tin

Preheat oven to a medium temperature (350°).
Beat the eggs and sugar, using an electric mixer at maximum speed, for about 7 minutes until pale and thick.
Gently fold in the hazelnuts and grated chocolate. Add matzoh-meal, mixed with baking powder, alternately with the orange juice and brandy.
Pour batter into a greased tin and bake in preheated oven for about 50 minutes.
Remove from oven and leave to cool. When cake is cold sprinkle with powdered sugar.

HAZELNUT AND BUTTER CAKE

INGREDIENTS:

6¹/₂ oz. butter
6¹/₂ oz. plain chocolate
5 eggs
1 cup sugar
6¹/₂ oz. hazelnuts, shelled,
    roasted and finely ground
2 tablespoons matzoh-meal
2 tablespoons brandy
1 tablespoon vanilla

A rectangular tin, two loaf tins,
    or a round 10 inch cake tin

Preheat oven to a medium temperature (350°).
Put butter and chocolate in a double boiler and heat over a low flame until melted.
Beat the eggs and sugar, using an electric mixer at maximum speed, for about 7 minutes or until pale and thick.
Gently fold in the ground nuts, matzoh-meal, brandy, vanilla and the chocolate mixture.
Pour into greased tin and bake in preheated oven for about 40 minutes.
Remove from oven and leave to cool. Sprinkle with powdered sugar, or spread with whipped cream flavored with sugar and a little instant coffee powder.

MOIST ORANGE CAKE

INGREDIENTS:

Pastry:
1¼ cups matzoh-meal*
4 eggs
¾ cup sugar
2 oz. almonds, shelled, roasted
 and finely ground
1½ teaspoons baking powder

*available before Passover in
Jewish specialty stores

Syrup:
1 cup sugar
3 tablespoons orange liqueur
1 cup orange juice, freshly
 squeezed

Topping:
½ cup apricot jam
1 cup whipping cream
2 teaspoons sugar

A rectangular 11x14 inch baking
 tin

Preheat oven to a medium heat (350°).
Finely grind matzoh-meal, using an electric blender.
Beat the eggs and sugar, using an electric mixer at maximum speed, for about 7 minutes until pale and thick.
Using a wooden spoon, fold in the ground matzoh-meal, ground almonds and baking powder.
Pour the batter into greased tin and bake in preheated oven for 15–20 minutes.
While cake is baking, boil the sugar, liqueur and orange juice to make syrup. Remove cake from the oven, pour the hot syrup on it and leave to cool.
Heat a little jam and spread on the cooled cake.
Beat the double cream with the sugar until stiff and spread on cake. Store in refrigerator.

SHAVUOT

CHEESECAKE

INGREDIENTS:

A real delight!

Pastry:
3 oz. margarine
2 tablespoons sugar
*Juice of 1 orange (or substitute 1
  egg yolk)*
1 cup self-rising flour

Filling:
*2x8 oz. packages and 1x3 oz.
  package cream cheese*
½ cup sugar
1 tablespoon lemon juice
2 tablespoons plain flour
1½ cups milk
2 egg yolks
1 teaspoon vanilla

Meringue Topping:
2 egg whites
¼ cup sugar

A round 10 inch cake tin

*Preheat oven to a medium temperature (350°).
Place pastry ingredients in a mixing bowl and knead to a smooth dough. Grease the tin and line its bottom and sides with the dough.
In a separate bowl, beat together the cheese, sugar, lemon juice, flour, milk, egg yolks and vanilla until smooth and creamy.
Pour the cheese mixture into dough-lined tin and bake in preheated oven for 35–45 minutes.
To make meringue topping, beat the egg whites, gradually adding the sugar, until stiff. Spread on the cheese filling, reduce oven temperature to low and bake for several minutes or until meringue is pale golden.*

APRICOT CHEESECAKE

INGREDIENTS:

Pastry:
1 egg
1/2 cup sugar
3 oz. margarine
1 cup self-rising flour

Filling:
15 apricots, fresh or canned
1 cup sugar
6 1/2 oz. butter
3 eggs, separated
1 1/2 lbs. cream cheese
1 cup whipping cream
1 tablespoon sugar
A little warmed jam to glaze

A square 12x12 inch baking tin
   or a 10 inch pie dish

Preheat oven to a medium temperature (350°).
In a mixing bowl, knead all pastry ingredients to a smooth and elastic dough.
Line the bottom and sides of a greased tin with the dough and bake in preheated oven for about 25 minutes. Remove from oven and leave to cool.
Meanwhile, if using fresh apricots, wash and drain them. Halve, stone, sprinkle with 1/2 cup of sugar and set aside for 15 minutes. If using canned apricots omit this stage.
In a mixing bowl, beat the butter and sugar, then beat in the egg yolks and cheese. In a separate bowl beat the egg whites until stiff. Fold into cheese mixture. Transfer the cheese mixture into the cooled shell.
Beat the cream, adding the sugar, until stiff and spread on the cheese filling. Place apricots, cut side up, on the whipped cream and brush with the warmed jam. Chill for several hours to allow the filling to set.

LEMON MERINGUE CHEESECAKE

INGREDIENTS:

4 eggs, separated
1½ cups sugar
1 lb. cream cheese
1 cup whipping cream
1 tablespoon semolina or 1
   tablespoon plain flour
5 oz. margarine, softened
2 tablespoons lemon juice
1 cup self-rising flour

Meringue Topping:
2 egg whites
¼ cup sugar

A round 11 inch cake tin

Preheat the oven to a medium temperature (350°).

Beat the egg whites until stiff, then add gradually 1 cup of the sugar.

In a separate bowl, beat together the egg yolks, remaining ½ cup of sugar, cheese, whipping cream, semolina or flour, margarine, lemon juice, vanilla and the flour until smooth and creamy.

Gently fold the beaten egg whites into cheese mixture. Pour the batter into a greased tin and bake in preheated oven for about 40 minutes.

Several minutes before removing the cake from the oven beat 2 egg whites with the sugar until stiff. Spread on top of the cake and continue baking until meringue is pale golden. Remove from oven, leave to cool and store in refrigerator.

STRIPED CHEESECAKE

INGREDIENTS:

This recipe uses only the egg yolks. The surplus egg whites may be used to bake a Rich Date Cake, which requires egg whites only.

Pastry:
3¹/₂ oz. margarine
4 tablespoons sugar
1 egg yolk
2¹/₂ cups self-rising flour
¹/₄ cup orange juice
1 egg, for brushing

Filling:
³/₄-1 cup sugar (to taste)
3 tablespoons lemon juice
4 egg yolks
1¹/₂ lbs. cream cheese
1 cup whipping cream

A round 10 inch cake tin

Preheat oven to a medium temperature (350°).
In a mixing bowl, knead all pastry ingredients to a smooth dough. Divide the dough into two equal parts and line the bottom and sides of a greased tin with one half. Reserve remaining dough.
Bake in preheated oven for about 20 minutes, or until the shell is half-baked.
Meanwhile beat all filling ingredients together until smooth and creamy.
Remove pastry shell from oven and pour filling into it.
Shape remaining half of the dough into long, narrow rolls and arrange on top of the filling in a lattice design. Brush with beaten egg and return to oven for a further 20 minutes. Remove from oven and leave to cool. Store in refrigerator.

EASY-TO-MAKE CHEESECAKE

INGREDIENTS:

Cheese Batter:
½ cup sugar
1 lb. cream cheese
1 egg
2 tablespoons lemon juice
1 tablespoon vanilla
⅓ cup milk

Egg Batter:
4 eggs
¾ cup sugar
1 tablespoon vanilla
1 tablespoon oil
1 tablespoon brandy
⅓ cup cornstarch
⅓ cup plain flour

Topping (optional):
⅔ cup sour cream
2 tablespoons sugar
2 tablespoons milk
1 tablespoon vanilla

A round 10 inch cake tin

Preheat oven to a medium temperature (350°).
To make cheese batter, beat together the sugar, cheese, egg, lemon juice, vanilla and milk until smooth.
To make egg batter, beat the eggs and sugar in a separate bowl, using an electric mixer at maximum speed, until pale and thick. Gradually fold in the vanilla, oil and brandy, then add the flour and cornstarch and fold with a wooden spoon.
Fold the egg batter into the cheese mixture, gently but thoroughly.
Pour the batter into a greased tin and bake in preheated oven for about 45 minutes.
To make topping (optional), beat all topping ingredients together until smooth. Spread on the cake and bake 2 more minutes.

INDIVIDUAL CHEESECAKES

INGREDIENTS:

If you do not own a muffin tin you may substitute it for paper cases (which need not be greased).

4 eggs, separated
¾ cup sugar
⅓ cup plain flour
⅓ cup cornstarch
1 teaspoon baking powder
8 oz. cream cheese
2 oz. margarine, melted
1 tablespoon vanilla

Topping:
1 cup whipping cream
1 tablespoon sugar
*Canned melon balls or apricot
   halves*

*A muffin tin or 18 individual
   cups*

Preheat oven to a medium temperature (300°).
Beat the egg whites, gradually adding the sugar, until stiff.
Sift together the flour, cornstarch and baking powder.
In a separate bowl, beat the cheese, margarine, vanilla and egg yolks until smooth and creamy.
Fold the cheese mixture and flour, alternately, into the beaten egg whites.
Pour the batter into a greased muffin tin and bake in preheated oven for 25 minutes. Remove from oven and leave to cool. The baked cakes will have a depression in the center.
To make topping, beat the whipping cream and sugar until stiff. Transfer to a piping bag and pipe a swirl of cream on every cake. Place a melon ball or half an apricot on each cake.

PLUM PIE

INGREDIENTS:

*This sweet and sour tasting pie
may be served hot or cold.*

Filling:
18 fresh plums
½ cup sugar (scant)

Pastry:
2½ cups plain flour
3½ oz. butter
1 small egg
¼ cup sugar

Topping:
3 egg whites
½ cup sugar

A 10 or 11 inch pie dish

*Halve and stone the plums, sprinkle with sugar
and set aside for half an hour.*
Preheat oven to a medium temperature (350°).
*In a mixing bowl, knead all dough ingredients
to a smooth dough. Line the bottom and sides
of a greased pie dish with a ⅛ inch thick layer of
dough.*
*Arrange the plums, cut side up, on the bottom
of the lined tin. Moisten the plums with a little
of the liquid which drained from them and bake
in preheated oven for about 20 minutes.*
*Meanwhile beat the egg whites, gradually
adding the sugar, until stiff. Spread the beaten
egg whites on top of the plums. Reduce oven
temperature to low and continue baking for a
further 10 minutes, until meringue is pale
golden.*

FRUIT FILLED CREAM ROLL

INGREDIENTS:

A light summer cake, filled with cream, for those who are not particularly enthusiastic about cheese cakes. The cake itself is a sponge roll, and should be baked at a medium temperature (350°) for no longer than 8 minutes, so that it is not too dry and can be easily rolled up. For a larger roll double the quantities and bake in a 14x16 inch baking tin. The quantities for the filling should remain the same.

Sponge Roll:
3 eggs, separated
½ cup sugar
1½ oz. margarine, melted
⅓ cup plain flour
2 tablespoons cornstarch
1 tablespoon vanilla
1 tablespoon brandy

Filling:
2 cups whipping cream
2 tablespoons sugar
3 tablespoons cream cheese
Pineapple or apricot slices, canned, drained and chopped
3½ oz. candied cherries (optional)

A rectangular 9½x13½ inch baking tin (small cookie sheet)

Line the tin with wax paper and grease with a little margarine. Preheat oven to a medium temperature.

Beat the egg whites, gradually adding the sugar, until stiff. Gently fold in the melted margarine. When margarine is completely incorporated, fold in the egg yolks, flour, cornstarch, vanilla and brandy.

Pour the batter into prepared tin and bake in preheated oven for about 8 minutes. Remove from oven and turn out on a clean dish towel, sprinkled with sugar. Peel off wax paper, roll the cake up in the towel and leave to cool.

To make filling, beat the whipping cream and sugar until stiff. Divide in two and fold the cheese into one portion of the cream.

Open up the rolled cake, spread with the cheese and cream mixture and arrange on top the pineapple or apricots and candied cherries.

Roll up again, spread with remaining cream and chill for several hours.

PLUM CAKE

INGREDIENTS:

An excellent coffee cake, ideal for a hot summer afternoon. The amount of sugar in the filling can be adjusted to individual taste.

Filling:
20 plums
About 6 tablespoons sugar

Batter:
6½ oz. butter, softened
1¾ cups sugar
4 eggs, separated
1 tablespoon vanilla
1 tablespoon lemon juice
1¾ cups self-rising flour

A rectangular 10x13 inch baking tin

Preheat oven to a medium temperature (350°). Halve and stone the plums. Sprinkle with sugar and set aside until batter is ready.
Beat together the margarine and 1 cup of sugar until smooth, then gradually beat in the egg yolks, vanilla, lemon juice and flour.
In a separate bowl beat the egg whites, gradually adding the remaining ¾ cup of sugar, until stiff. Gently fold the beaten egg whites into the yolk mixture until no trace of white remains. Pour the batter into a greased tin and arrange the halved plums on top. Bake in preheated oven for 40–50 minutes or until done.

MELON AND CREAM CHEESESAKE

INGREDIENTS:

A tasty, easy-to-make cake. The pastry can be prepared the day before. The crunchy melon adds flavor and moistness, but out of season it may be substituted with apples or canned pineapple.

Pastry:
5 oz. margarine
¹/₂ cup sugar
1 whole egg
1 egg yolk
2¹/₄ cups self-rising flour

Filling:
2 cups whipping cream
1¹/₂ lbs. cream cheese
1 cup sugar
¹/₂ oz. unflavored gelatine
¹/₃ cup boiling water
¹/₂ a small melon, cubed (about 1 lb.)

A rectangular 10x13 inch baking tin or 2 9x9 inch baking tins

Preheat oven to a medium temperature (350°).
In a mixing bowl, knead all pastry ingredients to a smooth dough. Line with the dough the bottom of a greased tin, and pull up a little to cover sides. The dough layer should be very thin (¹/₈ inch).
Bake in preheated oven until lightly browned, remove from oven and leave to cool.
Meanwhile, prepare the filling: Beat the whipping cream until stiff. In a separate bowl beat together the cheese and sugar.
Dissolve the gelatine in boiling water, heat a little and fold into the cheese. Fold the whipped cream into the cheese, pour the filling into the cooled shell and drop the melon cubes on it.
Chill for several hours, to allow filling to set.

CHOCOLATE COVERED CHEESECAKE

INGREDIENTS:

Pastry:
3½ oz. butter
½ cup sugar
1 whole egg
1 egg yolk
1½ cups self-rising flour

Filling:
4 eggs
1 tablespoon vanilla
1¼ cups sugar
1 tablespoon plain flour
3 tablespoons cornstarch
⅔ cup sour cream
¼ cup milk
1 lb. cream cheese

Chocolate Glaze:
½ cup water
½ cup sugar
6 oz. chocolate chips
1½ tablespoons cocoa powder,
* unsweetened*

A round 10 inch cake tin

Preheat oven to a medium temperature (350°).
In a mixing bowl knead all pastry ingredients to a smooth dough. Grease the tin and line the bottom and sides with dough.
Beat the eggs and sugar, using an electric mixer at maximum speed, for about 7 minutes or until pale and thick. Fold in remaining ingredients, using a wooden spoon. Pour into lined tin and bake in preheated oven for about 45 minutes. Remove from oven and leave to cool.
To make chocolate glaze, place sugar and water in a small saucepan and heat over a low flame until sugar is dissolved. Add chocolate chips and cocoa powder and beat until mixture thickens. Pour on top of cooled cake.

CREAM AND MELON SPONGE CAKE

INGREDIENTS:

A super-easy, delicious cake. When unexpected guests announce a visit, all you have to do is thaw the frozen sponge cake kept for just such an emergency, prepare the cream topping, and set the cake in the refrigerator to await the guests!

1 frozen sponge cake, thawed

1 cup whipping cream
3 tablespoons sugar
¼ cup cherry or orange liqueur
½ medium melon, peeled, seeded and thinly sliced
1 packet instant strawberry flavored Jello

Halve the cake and return one layer to the freezer, for future use.
Scoop out inside of cake, leaving a shell about 1 inch thick.
Beat the whipping cream with the sugar until stiff. Sprinkle the sherry or liqueur on the cake.
Fill the cake with the whipped cream. Arrange melon slices on the whipped cream.
Prepare Jello according to instructions on the packet, and let cool a little.
Carefully spoon Jello on the melon slices. Chill for several hours before serving.

SPECIAL OCCASIONS

POUND CAKE

INGREDIENTS:

The ideal cake for picnics or out of doors entertaining.

6 eggs, separated
1¾ cups sugar
5 oz. margarine
Juice of 1 large lemon
1 tablespoon vanilla
2½ cup self-rising flour
2 oz. walnuts, chopped

To Decorate:
Powdered sugar

A round 10 inch cake tin or 2 loaf tins

Preheat oven to a medium temperature (350°).
Beat the egg whites, gradually adding 1 cup of sugar, until stiff.
In a separate bowl beat the margarine with remaining sugar, egg yolks, lemon juice, vanilla, flour and walnuts, using an electric mixer at minimum speed.
Gently fold the beaten egg whites into the margarine mixture until thoroughly mixed.
Pour batter into a greased tin (or tins) and bake in preheated oven for 40–50 minutes. Remove from oven and leave to cool. When cold, sprinkle with powdered sugar.

CHOCOLATE MOUSSE CAKE

INGREDIENTS:

Try it – it's worth it! The cake is recommended for parties, although it should be kept chilled till serving time.

Cake:
2 large eggs
1/3 cup sugar
1 1/2 oz. margarine, melted
1 tablespoon cornstarch
1/2 cup plain flour
3 tablespoons brandy
2 tablespoons water
1/2 cup warmed apricot jam

Chocolate Mousse:
8 oz. plain chocolate
3 1/2 oz. butter
3 eggs, separated
1/2 cup sugar
1 cup whipping cream

To Decorate:
2 oz. hazelnuts, coarsely chopped

A 9x9 inch baking tin

Preheat oven to a medium temperature (350°).

Beat the eggs and sugar, using an electric mixer at maximum speed, until pale and thick.

Fold in the margarine, cornstarch and flour, using a wooden spoon. Pour the batter into a greased tin and bake in preheated oven for 15–20 minutes. Remove from oven and leave to cool.

Mix brandy and water and sprinkle on cake. Spread with warmed jam.

To make chocolate mousse, melt chocolate and margarine in a double boiler. When melted, remove from heat and gradually stir in the egg yolks.

In a separate bowl, beat the egg whites and sugar until firm. Add the melted chocolate to the beaten egg whites and gently fold together until no trace of white remains.

Beat the whipping cream until stiff, and fold half of the whipped cream into the chocolate mixture.

Spread the chocolate mousse on top of the cake and top with remaining cream. Chill for several hours before serving. To serve, sprinkle with chopped nuts.

DRIED FRUIT CAKE

INGREDIENTS:

3½ oz. margarine, softened
¾ cup sugar
3 eggs
1 cup self-rising flour
5 dried dates, chopped
1 tablespoon pine-kernels
2 oz. seedless raisins
3½ oz. dried apricots, chopped
3½ oz. plain chocolate, grated
1 tablespoon vanilla
2 oz. hazelnuts, shelled and
  halved
2 oz. walnuts, shelled

To Decorate:
Powdered sugar

A large loaf tin or two small loaf
  tins

Preheat oven to a medium temperature (350°).
In the mixer bowl, beat together the margarine and sugar until light and fluffy. Add the eggs, one at a time, beating well after each addition.
In a separate bowl mix the flour and dried friut, then stir into the margarine mixture.
Add the grated chocolate, vanilla and nuts.
Pour into a greased and floured tin and bake in preheated oven for about 40 minutes. Remove from oven and leave to cool. When cake is completely cooled sprinkle with powdered sugar.

CHOCOLATE CAKE

INGREDIENTS:

A delicious cake, suitable for Passover or any other festive occasion.

Cake batter:
6½ oz. plain chocolate
6 eggs, separated
½ cup sugar
3½ oz. butter, softened
3½ oz. nuts, finely ground
2 oz. nuts, chopped
2 tablespoons matzoh-meal

Topping:
1 packet chocolate cream
  topping, or
  1 cup whipping cream
2 teaspoons sugar
1 teaspoon instant coffee powder

Cream:
3½ oz. margarine, softened
3½ oz. powdered sugar
1 teaspoon instant coffee powder

A round 10 or 11 inch cake tin

Preheat oven to a medium temperature (350°).
Melt the chocolate in a double boiler placed over a low flame, stirring constantly.
Beat the egg whites, gradually adding half of the sugar, until stiff. In a separate bowl, beat the yolks with the remaining sugar and the butter until smooth.
Gradually beat the melted chocolate, nuts and matzoh-meal into the yolk mixture. Fold the chocolate mixture into the beaten egg whites carefully but thoroughly.
Reserve 1 cup of the chocolate mixture and store in refrigerator. Pour the rest of the batter into a greased tin and bake in preheated oven for about 35 minutes.
Remove from oven and spread the reserved chocolate mixture onto the hot cake. Chill.
Prepare the topping according to instructions, or beat the double cream with sugar and instant coffee powder until stiff (optional). Spread on the cake.
Beat the margarine, powdered sugar and instant coffee powder to a smooth cream and pipe on top of the cake, using a piping bag fitted with a star nozzle.

GERBEAUD SLICES (NUT LAYER CAKE)

INGREDIENTS:

This magnificent cake can be stored in the refrigerator or frozen. Although the dough includes yeast it should not be allowed to rise.

Pastry:
1/2 oz. yeast
1/2 cup sugar
8 oz. butter or margarine
3 cups flour
3 tablespoons sour cream
1 egg
Pinch of salt

Filling:
10 oz. nuts, ground
8 oz. sugar
1 1/4 cups apricot jam

Shiny Glaze:
1/2 cup water
1/2 cup sugar
6 1/2 oz. plain chocolate
1 1/2 tablespoons cocoa powder

A small cookie sheet or an 11x17
   inch baking tin

Preheat oven to a medium temperature (350°). Blend the yeast with a little sugar. Place the rest of the pastry ingredients in a mixing bowl and add the yeast. Knead to a smooth, soft dough. Divide dough into three balls.

Roll out one dough ball on a floured board to a large rectangle. Wrap loosely around rolling pin, and spread over bottom of a greased tin.

Mix the ground nuts with the sugar. Spread the dough in the tin with jam and sprinkle with half of the nut mixture. Roll out another rectangle, cover the nut layer, spread with jam and sprinkle with the remaining nut mixture. Roll out the remaining dough, place on top of the nut layer and bake for about 30 minutes, or until golden. Remove from oven and leave to cool.

To make shiny glaze, put water and sugar in saucepan and heat until sugar is dissolved. Add the chocolate and stir until melted. Add cocoa powder and beat until thickens. Pour on cooled cake. To serve, cut into diamonds.

CHOCOLATE MARZIPAN CAKE

INGREDIENTS:

This lovely, heart-shaped cake is a favorite treat for children.

Cake batter:
1¾ cups self-rising flour
4 tablespoons cocoa powder, unsweetened
1 teaspoon instant coffee powder
4½ oz. margarine
1½ cups sugar
3 eggs
1 tablespoons vanilla
2 tablespoons brandy
½ cup milk

¼ cup sweet red wine

Topping:
½ cup apricot jam
6½ oz. almond paste
Sugared flowers or bought almond paste flowers
Silver balls

A round 10 inch cake tin, or a heart-shaped tin

Preheat oven to a medium temperature (350°).
Sift together flour, cocoa powder and instant coffee powder.
In the mixer bowl, beat margarine and sugar at minimum speed until light and fluffy. Gradually beat in the eggs, one at a time, then the vanilla and brandy.
Alternately add the flour mixture and milk, beating well after each addition.
Pour batter into greased and floured tin and bake in preheated oven for 40 minutes. Remove from oven and leave to cool.
Halve the cake and sprinkle the bottom half with the wine, diluted with a little water. Spread with apricot jam and cover with the top half of the cake.
On a board sprinkled with powdered sugar, roll out the almond paste to fit the cake and place on top of the cake.
Decorate with bought sugar or almond paste flowers, silver balls etc.

APPLE POUND CAKE

INGREDIENTS:

This cake is so easy it can be made by children.

6½ oz. margarine
1 cup sugar
3 eggs
⅔ cup buttermilk
2¾ cups self-rising flour
½ teaspoon ground cinnamon
1 tablespoon vanilla
*4 cooking apples, peeled and
  cored*

2 loaf tins

Preheat oven to a medium temperature (300°).
Place the margarine, sugar and eggs in mixing bowl and beat at minimum speed until light and fluffy.
Alternately add the flour and buttermilk, then beat in the cinnamon and vanilla. Beat until smooth.
Cube or thinly slice the apples and fold into the batter, using a wooden spoon.
Pour the batter into greased tins and bake in preheated oven for about 40 minutes.
To test if cake is ready, insert the tip of a knife or a wooden skewer into center of cake. If the knife or skewer comes out clean, the cake is baked.

EASY-TO-MAKE CHOCOLATE CAKE

INGREDIENTS:

Cake Batter:
6 oz. margarine
1½ cups sugar
3 eggs
2¼ cups self-rising flour
4 tablespoons cocoa powder,
  unsweetened
1 cup milk
1 teaspoon instant coffee powder
1 tablespoon vanilla

Chocolate Glaze:
4 tablespoons sugar
4 tablespoons water
6½ oz. plain chocolate, chopped
4 tablespoons margarine

A round 10 inch cake tin

Preheat oven to a medium temperature (350°).
Place the margarine, sugar and eggs in a mixing bowl and beat at minimum speed until smooth. Sift together the flour and cocoa powder. Alternately add the flour mixture and milk to the margarine mixture, beating well after each addition. Add the instant coffee powder and vanilla and beat again.
Pour the batter into a greased tin and bake in preheated oven for about 40 minutes.
While cake is baking, prepare the glaze: Put sugar and water in a small saucepan and bring to a boil over a low flame. Add the chocolate and stir. When melted, remove from flame, add margarine and stir until smooth.
Remove cake from oven and leave to cool. Spread the glaze on top of the cooled cake. Sprinkle silver balls or chopped nuts on top, if wished.

WHIPPED CREAM LAYER CAKE

INGREDIENTS:

Cake Batter:
8 eggs
1½ cups sugar
6½ oz. margarine, melted
1 tablespoon vanilla
2 cups plain flour
1 tablespoon cocoa powder,
    unsweetened

Syrup:
½ cup sugar
¾ cup water
½ cup cooking sherry

Filling:
3½ oz. nuts, finely chopped
3½ oz. candied cherries,
    chopped
1 small can peach or apricot
    halves, drained and chopped

Topping:
3 cups whipping cream
3 tablespoons sugar

To Decorate:
grated chocolate

3 round 9 inch cake tins

Line three 9 inch cake tins with wax paper. Preheat oven to medium (350°).

To make cake, beat the eggs and sugar, using an electric mixer at maximum speed, for about 9 minutes or until pale and thick. Gently fold in the melted margarine. Add the vanilla and flour and fold gently but thoroughly. Divide the batter into three equal parts. Pour two parts into two lined tins. Sprinkle the cocoa powder on the third part, fold in and pour into the third tin. Bake each layer for about 20 minutes.

Meanwhile, prepare the syrup. Place water and sugar in a small saucepan and cook, stirring, for 5 minutes. Add the sherry. Remove cakes from oven, turn out and peel off wax paper. Place a white layer on a cake tray and sprinkle with a third of the syrup. Cover with a third of the ground nuts and the cherries.

Beat the whipping cream with the sugar until stiff and spread a third of the whipped cream on the cake. Cover with the chocolate cake layer and repeat spreading syrup, nuts, cherries, whipped cream and some chopped peaches or apricots. Top with the last layer, spread with remaining whipped cream and decorate with grated chocolate or sliced peaches and cherries.

MARZIPAN CREAM CUPS

INGREDIENTS:

Pastry:
4 eggs
¾ cup sugar
1 tablespoon vanilla
1 tablespoon brandy
⅓ cup plain flour
⅓ cup cornstarch

Filling:
1 cup whipping cream
2 tablespoons sugar
1 tablespoon instant coffee
  powder
6½ oz. almond paste

To Decorate:
Hundreds and thousands of
  sprinkles

A small cookie sheet

Preheat oven to a medium-high temperature (375°).

Place the eggs and sugar in the mixer bowl and beat at maximum speed for about 7 minutes, until pale and thick. Gently fold in the vanilla, brandy, flour and cornstarch.

Line a tin with wax paper. Pour the batter into prepared tin and bake in preheated oven for 15-20 minutes. Remove from oven and leave to cool.

Meanwhile, beat the whipping cream, gradually adding sugar and instant coffee powder, until it holds soft peaks.

Cut circles out of the baked cake, using a 2-inch pastry cutter, and place on a tray. Transfer the whipped cream into a piping bag fitted with a plain nozzle, and pipe a swirl of cream on each circle.

Roll out the almond paste on a board lightly sprinkled with powdered sugar. Cut into strips 2 inches wide and 6 inches long. Wrap the almond paste strips around the pastry circles and store in refrigerator.

CREAM AND RASPBERRIES CHOCOLATE CAKE

INGREDIENTS:

The raspberries may be substituted for strawberries or cherries.

Cake Batter:
4 eggs
³/₄ cup sugar
³/₄ cup plain flour
¹/₃ cup cocoa powder,
   unsweetened
1 tablespoon vanilla
3¹/₂ oz. margarine, melted

Syrup:
¹/₈ cup sugar
¹/₂ cup water
¹/₈ cup cooking sherry

Apricot jam for glazing

Topping:
1 cup whipping cream
2 tablespoons sugar
10 oz. raspberries, fresh or
   frozen and thawed

A round 10 inch cake tin

Preheat oven to a medium temperature (350°).
Place eggs and sugar in the mixer bowl and beat at maximum speed for 5–7 minutes, until pale and thick.
Sift together the flour and cocoa powder. Gently fold the flour mixture, vanilla and melted margarine into the beaten eggs.
Pour the batter into a greased tin and bake in preheated oven for about 30 minutes. Remove from oven and leave to cool.
Meanwhile prepare the syrup: place sugar and water in a small saucepan and bring to a boil over a low flame. Cook for 5 minutes, until sugar is dissolved. Remove from heat and add the sherry.
Pour the syrup on the cooled cake. Heat the jam (for easier spreading) and spread on the cake. Leave to cool.
Beat the whipping cream with the sugar until it forms soft peaks, spread on the cooled cake, then scatter the raspberries, or any other fruit on top.

CHOCOLATE CHERRY CAKE

INGREDIENTS:

4 eggs
¾ cup sugar
3½ oz. margarine, melted
¾ cup plain flour
½ cup cocoa powder,
   unsweetened
⅛ cup brandy
⅛ cup tea

Filling:
1 cup whipping cream
1 tablespoon sugar
3½ oz. candied cherries or
   canned pineapple, chopped

A rectangular 9x13 inch baking
   tin

Preheat oven to a medium temperature (350°).
Place eggs and sugar in the mixer bowl and beat at maximum speed for about 7 minutes, until pale and thick.
Gradually pour the melted margarine into the beaten eggs, stirring with a wooden spoon. Finally fold in the flour and cocoa powder.
Pour the batter into a greased tin and bake in preheated oven for about 20 minutes. Remove from oven and leave to cool. When cold cut cake lengthwise and place on a serving dish.
Blend brandy and tea and moisten one half of the cake with the mixture.
To make filling, beat the whipping cream and sugar until it holds in soft peaks. Spread the whipped cream on the moistened half of the cake, and sprinkle the chopped cherries on top.
Cover with remaining half of the cake, sprinkle a little of the brandy mixture, spread with whipped cream and arrange remaining cherries on top.
Chill for several hours before serving. Store chilled.

FESTIVE CREAM CAKE

INGREDIENTS:

Cake Batter:
10 oz. plain chocolate
1½ oz. butter
6 eggs, separated
½ cup sugar + 2 tablespoons
   sugar
1 tablespoon brandy
1 tablespoon breadcrumbs
2 teaspoons instant coffee
   powder

Chocolate Cream:
1 cup sugar
2 tablespoons cocoa powder,
   unsweetened or 3½ oz. plain
   chocolate
½ cup water
1 teaspoon vanilla
1 teaspoon rum or brandy
3½ oz. butter, softened
2 egg yolks

Topping (optional):
1 cup whipping cream
1 tablespoon sugar

A round 10 inch cake tin

Preheat oven to a medium temperature (350°).
Place the chocolate and butter in a double boiler and stir until melted. Allow to cool.
Beat the egg whites until they foam, then add ½ a cup of sugar and continue beating until stiff.
Place the yolks in a separate double boiler and add 2 teaspoons sugar. Heat, beating constantly with a hand mixer, until mixture thickens a little. Set aside to cool.
Beat the yolk mixture into the chocolate.
Fold the chocolate mixture into the beaten egg whites. Add the brandy, breadcrumbs and instant coffee powder and fold gently but thoroughly. Pour batter into a greased tin and bake for about 30 minutes. Remove from oven and cool.
Meanwhile, prepare the chocolate cream: place the sugar, cocoa powder and water in a saucepan. Cook over a low flame. Add vanilla and rum or brandy.
Beat the butter and egg yolks until smooth. Add the cooled chocolate syrup and beat to a smooth cream. Chill. Spread the cold chocolate cream on top of the cake.
Whipped cream topping (optional): Beat whipping cream and sugar and spread on the chocolate cream.

SACHER TORTE

INGREDIENTS:

This magnificent cake is named after the famous Hotel Sacher in Vienna.

6½ oz. plain chocolate
3½ oz. butter
3½ oz. margarine, softened
1½ cups sugar
5 eggs, separated
1 tablespoon vanilla
1 tablespoon brandy
¾ cup milk
1½ cups self-rising flour
2 tablespoons breadcrumbs
1 tablespoon cornstarch
½ cup homemade jam

Glaze :
½ cup water
½ cup sugar
6½ oz. chocolate chips
1½ tablespoons cocoa powder, unsweetened

A round 10 inch cake tin

Prepare the cake a day before serving. Preheat the oven to a medium temperature (350°).
Melt chocolate in a double boiler.
Place the butter, margarine and half of the sugar in the mixer bowl and beat at minimum speed. Gradually beat in the egg yolks, vanilla, brandy, melted chocolate and finally the milk.
In a separate bowl beat the egg whites with the remaining sugar until firm.
Fold the chocolate mixture into the beaten egg whites. Finally, fold in the flour, breadcrumbs and cornstarch.
Pour the batter into a greased tin and bake in preheated oven for 45–60 minutes. Chill overnight.
The next day cut the cake into three layers and spread each layer with jam.
To make glaze: *Place water and sugar in a saucepan and heat until sugar dissolves. Add chocolate chips and stir over a low flame until melted. Add the cocoa powder and stir until thickens (about 2 minutes).*

CHOCOLATE BUTTER CAKE

INGREDIENTS:

The chocolate cream for this delicious cake has to be prepared a day in advance, and beaten the next day like plain whipping cream.

Chocolate Cream:
1 cup whipping cream
3½ oz. chocolate chips

Cake:
6½ oz. plain chocolate
5 eggs, separated
8 oz. butter, softened
8 oz. powdered sugar
3 tablespoons breadcrumbs
4 tablespoons good-quality brandy

A round 10 inch cake tin

Prepare the chocolate cream the day before: place the whipping cream and the chocolate chips in a saucepan. Bring to a boil over a low flame, remove from heat and chill for 24 hours.

The next day, prepare the cake: preheat oven to a medium temperature (350°). Melt chocolate in a double boiler.

Place yolks, butter and 4 oz. of the powdered sugar in the mixer bowl. Beat at minimum speed and gradually add the melted chocolate, breadcrumbs and brandy. Beat until smooth.

In a separate bowl beat the egg whites and remaining sugar until stiff. Gently fold into chocolate mixture.

Pour into a greased baking tin and bake in preheated oven for about 40 minutes. Remove from oven and leave to cool.

Remove chilled cream from refrigerator and beat until it holds soft peaks. Spread the whipped chocolate cream on the cooled cake.

HAZELNUT CREAM SHORTCAKE

INGREDIENTS:

This cake has to be prepared a day in advance and stored in the fridge.

Pastry:
1 egg
1¾ cups plain flour
3½ oz. butter
½ cup sugar

Hazelnut Cream:
2 cups whipping cream
2 tablespoons sugar
5 oz. hazelnuts, finely ground

To Decorate:
Grated chocolate

A round 10 inch cake tin

Preheat oven to a medium temperature (350°).
In a mixing bowl knead all pastry ingredients to a smooth, firm dough.
Divide dough into three equal parts. Mark on wax paper three circles, 10 inches in diameter, using the bottom of a cake tin. Roll out each part of the dough to fit the circles. Bake each circle separately in preheated oven for about 25 minutes. Remove from oven and leave to cool.
Beat the whipping cream until it holds soft peaks, then fold in the sugar and ground nuts.
Sandwich the pastry layers together with the whipped cream, and finish with a whipped cream layer.
Sprinkle grated chocolate on top and store in refrigerator.

HOLIDAY NUT CAKE

INGREDIENTS:

Cook chocolate cream a day in advance, refrigerate overnight and beat to a cream the next day.

Chocolate Cream:
1 cup whipping cream
2 tablespoons sugar
5 oz. chocolate chips

Cake Batter:
6½ oz. butter, softened
1¼ cups sugar
5 eggs, separated
6½ oz. plain chocolate, grated
6½ oz. nuts, finely ground
½ cup chocolate flavored
  self-rising flour (add 1
  tablespoon cocoa powder to
  flour)

Topping:
Cooked chocolate cream or
  powdered sugar
A little apricot jam

A shallow, rectangular 9½x13½ inch cookie sheet

The day before serving, prepare the chocolate cream – place the whipping cream, sugar and chocolate chips in a saucepan and bring to a boil over a low flame. Remove from heat and chill for 24 hours.

The next day, preheat oven to a medium temperature (350°).

Place butter and 1 cup of the sugar in mixer bowl and beat until light and fluffy.

Gradually beat in the yolks. Add the grated chocolate and ground nuts and stir.

Beat the egg whites, gradually adding the remaining sugar, until stiff. Gently fold the flour into the beaten egg whites.

Add the chocolate mixture into the beaten egg whites and fold until no trace of the whites remains. Pour into a greased tin and bake in preheated oven for about 30 minutes. Remove from oven and spread with a little apricot jam. Leave to cool.

Remove chocolate cream from refrigerator and beat until it forms soft peaks. Spread on top of the cake.

Variation: *The cake may also be assembled in layers (as shown in photograph): cut cake in half, sandwich both halves with jam and cream and spread top of cake with remaining jam and cream.*

INDEX

©1996 MODAN Publishing House

Printed in Israel